The Bees of the Horizon

The Bees of the Horizon

XII Poems
From the French

translated
by

Fred Beake

Paul Valéry

TOMBS BY THE SEA

Quiet roof, where doves stroll by pines
and there is palpitation of tombs.
Noon brings her justice, the ocean is flame,
sea that has begun again and again.
True reward for meditation
on the calm of immortality!

What pure work's delicate light
devours each diamond of imperceptible foam,
what self conceiving peace.
When the titan sun rests over the abyss
— pure works from eternal beginnings,
Time scintillates, and to dream is to know.

Unshifting treasure, shrine devote to Minerva,
great calm, visible withholding,
haughty water, eye maintaining
deep slumber under a wing of fire:
the silence of self: soul's edifice
— gathering together of a thousand gold tiles —

roof, temple to Time, that a sigh resumes,
clear point I clamber to and acclimatise
surrounded by my seaward gaze;
supreme offering to Heaven,
quiet scintillation on the height
that sows a sovereign disdain.

As fruit dissolves in pleasure
and delightfully changes its absence
in a mouth where its appearance dies,
I taste the smoke of my future,
and sky declaims to a soul that is consumed
rumours of a shifting coastline.

Frail sky, true sky, behold my transformation!
Pride has passed; there is such strange quietude.
It is so full of potency. I give myself up
to this shining place, and my shadow moves over
the houses of the Dead. I sense its frail motion!

My soul is bare to the flames of midday.
I have to uphold you, appropriate Justice.
Light now present and merciless
I deliver to your first pure place.
See yourself! But to restore the light
provisos a weary other half of shadow.

I am alone, wholly alone,
by the beating of a heart, and the springs of the poem,
in between void and pure event,
waiting for the echo from my inner immensity
— shadowy, harsh, rumbling cistern
noising in the soul what is yet to come.

Are you aware, false captive of leaves,
depth nibbling at these little bits of metal,
embarrassing secrets over my eyes,
what body drags me to achieve nothing,
what face draws it to this earth of bones?
My dead ones are just a glimmer there.

Fire without matter, sacred, set apart,
remains of earth offered to light,
I take pleasure in this place your fires dominate.
It is composed of gold, stone, and dark trees.
What great marble shivers over my shadows.
What sea slumbers faithfully over my tombs.

You fine bitch, away with your idolatry.
I am alone with a shepherd's grin,
keeping strange flocks a long lifetime,
keeping the white flock of the still tombs,
avoiding the precision of doves,
pointless dreams and the inquisition of angels.

Now I am here the future is quietness.
Sharp insects grate on dryness.
All's burnt, undone and taken into air
to a painful essence none can know...
Life — hunger, Being — drunk on absence,
bitterness becomes sweet, and spirit clear.

The hidden dead are alright in the soil.
It gives them warmth, and dries out their mystery.
Noon is high in the sky, noon is motionless,
thinking to itself alone, and sufficient to itself...
head of completion, diadem of perfection,
I am in you the change and the mystery.

There is only me to contain your fears.
What I respect, my doubts, my constraints
these are the flaws of your diamond.
But among the tree roots a quivering kind
have made your slow choice already,
though it is dark, and marble weighs them down.

They have dissolved in the depth of absence,
red clay has drunk the white species,
and their life is passed into flowers.
Where are the dead, the words of each one,
their individual skill and particular souls.
The worm glides where their tears rolled.

The shrieking of girls being tormented is shrill.
Teeth, eyes, and wet eyelids are busy.
Their lovely breasts play with fire.
The blood is redder in lips that yield.
But these pass under the earth,
with their final surrender, and the fingers
that try not to yield; and yet they return to the fray.

And so, great soul, we expect a vision, do we?
— that lacks the lie's shading, that ocean
and the gold light create for human eyes.
Will you declaim when you are mere gas?
Go! Everything passes. My presence has holes in it.
Holy impatience dies as well!

Immortality is meagre, black and gilded,
and has the alarming consolation of laurel.
This makes of death a mother's breast
— a nice lie, and a pleasant ruse.
But who is not aware, or can refuse
brainless skull and eternal grin?

Earth-deep fathers, empty skulls,
weighed down by shovelfulls, nevertheless
you are the earth, and confuse our steps.
Realistic rodent., and irrefutable worm
have no place with you, who are asleep
under the table. You saw life
and never leave me.

Is it self love or self hate.
His secret tooth is near
and any name approximates.
So what? He sees, desires, dreams, touches.
He likes my flesh, and even asleep
I live to be part of this live being.

Zeno! Cruel Zeno! Zeno of Elea
Have you pierced me with this winged shaft,
that quivers, flies, and fails to fly…
I hear it, and am a child. The shaft slays me.
Ah, the sun. What tortoise shade for the soul?
Achilles strides forward, but is suddenly still.

No! No! To the next era!
Body break this way of thinking.
Drink breath of the wind's birth.
There is a breath from the sea, freshness
that restores my soul. Oh the force of the salt ocean!
Let us rush to the sea and emerge living!

Great ocean, dowered with delirium,
panther's skin, cloak full of holes
that display a thousand images of sun,
hydra, all hydra, drunk in your blue flesh,
nibbling at your shimmering tail
in a clamouring of silence

the wind rises. We have got to try and live!
Great winds out of heaven turn the pages of my book
and shut it again. Waves grind rocks
and regurgitate them. Fly, embarrassed pages!
Break waves! Shatter the quiet roof
of joyous waters where dove-sails pecked!

Louis Aragon

LILACS AND ROSES 1940

Month of blossom, month of changes,
May without clouds, June full of daggers
— I'll not forget the lilacs and the roses
or those that the Spring in her skirts has folded

I'll not forget that horrible illusion
— procession, shouting of the crowd in the sun,
tanks full of the love and gifts of Belgium,
air trembling, bees in murmuration,
reckless triumph that began the fight,
blood foretold in the kisses' pink,
those to die upright in tank turrets,
garlanded with lilacs by a thankful people.

I'll not forget the gardens of France
(like missals of bygone ages)
or the troubled night's uncertain silence
(roses all along the road we had travelled through)
madness of those blossoms in the wind of panic
to soldiers flying on the wing of fear,
wild cyclists and ironic guns
and the refugees bleak terror.

But why does this storm of images
bring me always back to the same place:
Sainte-Marthe — a general — black branches,
a Norman villa in woodland — a certain peace,
for the foe are resting in the shadows.
Someone says "Paris has surrendered tonight".
Oh I'll not forget the lilacs and the roses
or the two loved ones that we lost.

Bouquet of the first day lilacs of Flanders,
sweet blossoms in the shadow whose death reddened cheeks,
and you bouquets of retreat, you Anjou roses
— the same colour as the incendiaries.

Rene Char

ARTINE
(To the silence of one who leaves off dreaming)

In the bed that had been made ready for me there was: a bloodied murdered creature with the remains of a bun, a pipe of lead, a gust of wind, iced lobster, unrolled scroll, two glove fingers, an oil stain; no prison door but the taste of bitterness, industrial diamond, dog, hair, broken chair, a silk worm, and something stolen, a chain from above, a tame fly that was green, a branch of coral, a cobbler's nail, a bus wheel.

Offering a glass of water in mid passage to a stricken horseman riding flat out — imagine that — on a race track (it might be a roman circus) overrun by the crowd with everywhere a total want of courtesy; Artine brought to souls she visited a like monumental uncouthness.

The restless one was keeping perfect count of the dreams that would haunt his brain hereafter, especially in the realm of lovers, where the consuming deed easily showed beyond sexual time; assimilation, self growing in the night into well-dressed ranks.

Artine without trouble traverses the name of a town. This, the silence that unbinds sleep.

The objects that have been designed and assembled as "true to nature" are part of the scenery in which the erotic acts of fatal issues are unfolded, that night and day epic. The warm, imaginary worlds that ceaselessly revolve in the country in the season of grains make the eye aggressive and loneliness unbearable to anyone with the power to destroy. To attain to strange upheavals it is preferable to surrender entirely to them.

The state of lethargy that preceded Artine had elements that were quite inseparable of piercing impressions upon the screen of drifting ruin: eiderdown cast down in flames into the shadowed, soundless abysm to perpetual motion.

Despite animals and storms Artine retained an untarnishable freshness. On the Pier this was utter transparence.

Surging to beauty in the worst depressions the apparition of the loveliness of Artine, the curious spirits dwell with the angry, the uncaring with the most curious.

The apparitions of Artine used to surpass the frames of those dream-lands where "For" and "For" are filled with equally murderous violence. They revolved in the folds of a burning silk dress peopled with trees whose leaves were of ash.

The cart that had been washed and sent back at nine carried him nearly always to the tapestried flat of saltpetre where eagerly gathered for interminable discussion the host of the mortal foes of Artine. The deadwood face especially was hateful. The racing breath of two lovers at risk from the mainroads became suddenly a large enough distraction to let the drama once again unfold itself to the open sky.

Sometimes a clumsy movement made slip on Artine's throat a head that wasn't mine. The enormous mass of suffering was then slowly consumed without smoke, presence in self and vibrant stillness.

The open book on Artine's knees could only be read on dark days. At irregular intervals the heroes came to learn the misfortunes that would fall anew on them, the various and harsh ways their faultless destiny was going to be entered upon. Uniquely concerned with Fatality they were for the most part of a pleasing build. They were slow to depart, indeed proved rather talkative. They expressed themselves by great unpredictable nods of the head. Each seemed to ignore himself when with the others,

The Poet's shot his model!

Rene Char

THE SHE OF HISTORY

    She sprinkles gold across the corn
    Splits its ear
    Nibbles the poles
    And dozes in the earth's flame

    The powerless look on the quarryman's face
    Hurled live in the lime
    Suffocated by a woman's eyes
    Her back quivering veins
    Lips a stream
    Joy huge

    All that removes itself convulsively from oneness with the world
    Detached from the whole by a child's simple push
    And covering us so very quickly
    We who do not confuse what's to be with what's been
    And do not know to ask in prayer
    Or to gain by pretence
    Who see night for lack of a woman's shoulder
    And day in pleasure's unfolding

In an indifferent heaven
The red bird of metals flies
Embellishing being
And my love's memory silently resumes its place
In the dust.

Rene Char

FORCE OF MILDNESS

I know where my inadequacies fetter me, stained glass if the bloom is snipped off from the blood of the summer's youth. Night's blackwater heart has taken the place of the sun, and the place of my heart. This evening the great wheel wandering so heavy with desire could well only be visible to me ... So am I always to know ruin, and only the places be different?

Rene Char

THE TOR

In the path that was numbed by grass, where we children wondered that the night dared pass, the wasps went no more in the brambles, and no birds in the branches. The air was opening to the hosts of the morning its wild immensity. There was just the filaments of wings, temptation to cry out, trapezing between light and transparence. The Tor was bright upon the lyre of its rocks. Mount Ventoux, mirror of eagles, lay in view.

In the path, numbed by grasses, the ghost of a lost age was smiling at our young tears.

Rene Char

CUR SECESSISTI

Snow, child's caprice, sun that have only the winter to shine in, to the door of my stone cell come, have shelter. On the slopes of Aulan my sons who are incendiary bombs, my sons who are killed with their eyes open, increase your power.

Rene Char

ANGUISH, EXPLOSION, SILENCE

Calavan Mill. Two years farm of cicadas, stronghold of owls. Here once was torrential speech, and soon after the laughter and struggles of children. Today the old rebel fails among its stones, mostly dead with ice, loneliness and zeal. In their turn the portents of the flowers are lulled in the silence. Roger Bernard: the monsters of the horizon lay too close to his earth.

Seek not on the mountain; but if a few miles thence in the gorges of Oppedette, you should meet lightning with the face of a scholar, go to it, oh go to it, and look favourably upon it, for it ought to be hungry, hungry for friendship.

Rene Char

PENUMBRA

I was in one of those forests where the sun has no access, but where, in the night the stars penetrate. This place had no right to exist, for the inquisition of parliaments had neglected it. The bonds that had been put by showed me their scorn. The shame of punishment had gone from me. In a small corner the memory of an old strength was caressing the peasant fugue of the grass. I governed myself without doctrine and with serene vehemence. I was the equal of the things whose secret lay beneath the flash of a wing. For the most part the essential has never been born, and those who possess it cannot exchange it without denying themselves. No thing will give up what it has gained, impaled on the point of its own pain. Without that all would be youth and grace, source and delta have the same purity.

I was in one of those forests where the sun has no access, but where (by night) the stars penetrate for implacable hostilities.

Robert Desnos

THE NIGHT OF LOVELESS NIGHTS

Most grim night wild with chill and decay
    With sick ghost and addled plant
Night of incandescence when fire flames in the wells
    Full of black shadows lies and treacheries

Who is it watches me through the mutterings of the waters?
    They are the ocean's victims. Remove
The tumour's curse from the skin of the flitting shadows.
    Their eyes have seen me. Stop their crying!

The Sun that day was dozing in the city.
    The shadow of chestnut trees lay before the buildings
Standards flopped on towers and the Summer piled
    Her fruits for the annual sacrifice.

Obviously vomiter of serpents, you come from a far land.
    Here the lover without sorrow vanishes
That's beyond doubt gloomy murderer. And you, suicide,
    Child of your works, would you blush, desiring joy?

When the night is long phantom it is my image
    That Love cooks and rehashes like a bad mushroom
Or the shadow of a woman in the hands of an impotent
    Among the cold coffins and vile hearts.

Yet I do not number you among them I disdain.
    Let's shake brother and embrace
Among the love letters, the combs and the ribbons.
    You never sullied your knees by prayer.

You were searching the sands beneath the sheer cliffs
    For the cove where the sailor stars shall make their landfall.
It was in the evening and fires were sailing the frosty sky.
    You were imagining among the saltpans

Watching nameless shiplike birds in plashings
   Of impossible fallings. Where are those evenings?
Reload your broadsides galleon waves. The wailing
   Heaven is full of targets. Oh

By what fate were you enchained to the service of the harsh,
   Of those whose hair is the delight of the hummingbird,
Of those whose hard firm breasts are a fatal hideaway,
   Of those whose nape is a nest of mystery

Of those whom you met naked in nights of disaster
   Some from the fire, some from the desert
Of those whom love branded before their due time
   Of those who maintain lies with truthful eyes

And these of the kind heart, and these of lovely limbs,
   Of these whose smile gleams with untruth's subtlety
And those whose love is a diamond agleam,
   Of those whose loins sway as they walk

Those whose thighs are gripped by tight shorts
   And of those who wear white silk knickers
Under their skirts, deliberately leaving a little skin free
   Between their garter and the sea of their flounces:

These whom you followed in hope or in doubt
   These whom you followed were not turning back
And the faded bouquets they tossed down as they went
   Long dragged you aimless in their footsteps

A rose in their mouths, their eyes tender
   They'll strive — and their hands are cruel —
To torture your heart and to spill your blood:
   So your champion's reward will be punishment

And you'll be lucky if it's enough to gain their love
   To meet unflinching wond'rous dangers
And keep your body and soul always faithful
   — And all to read affection in their eyes —

But the boldest, if not the most sincere
    Steal a promise from our lips to theirs
Their smiles gleaming and their hair waving
    Before our minds like figureheads before ships

For Love and his sorrows is sole monarch
    And holds the possession of the lover's heart
Some misfortune has brought beneath his law
    Have known only the hangman many years

And others have followed after him in his transformations:
    After the deep blue eyes come
The black shimmering in a face where the rose fades deeper
    Than either Heaven or despair

Master of their sleeping and of their waking
    He drags them en masse across country
Towards disembowelled oceans and ghastly meetings . . .
    The tide shall be full and the star has fallen.

My friend told me how he saw pass
    Lost in the ice in a chaos of hills
And far from all oceans, noiseless and smokeless
    A huge, flag-decked liner

And sailors leaned in silence on the ropes
    And birds wheeled over the bulwarks screeching
And women dancers stood beside the bulwarks in turban
    And evening gown wrapt in dream

Necks and wrists had an icy aura of jewels
    The big feathery fans in their hands
Waved towards the ports and the blushing
    Of church tower and entrance

And male dancers stood lost deep in melancholy
    Silently comparing their dears to steel.
It was in the mountains on an evening of madness
    When great clouds flowed down the glaciers

And another friend found in a hollow clearing
    A blossoming rose in the midst of firs . . .
And how many did he pick of those gay roses
    Before he fell asleep beneath the moss in the mornings

But his eyes kept the inscription of that
    Weird scene upon their pupils. Uncertain
His heart chose to cease its beating convictionless
    In that place of the scent of the rose and thyme.

From the time of our singing with vibrant voices
    We traversed those most singular countries
Where echo replied to the questionings of lovers
    With words whose sense we knew

But since the night fell down upon our heads
    The words have strange overtones in our hearts
And when sometimes memory makes them return on us
    We would disobey their imperious order.

Do you hear the singing deep among the mountains
    Remember the echoing cry of hunting horn and bucsin?
Why do we sing only the songs of the convict
    To the sound of an eternal gloomy tocsin?

Oughtn't this to be Don Juan who comes wandering down these lanes
    Where shadows wed with lovers' ghosts?
This footstep that echoes through the dark's desolations
    Has it bruised their hearts with its heavy heel?

Not the Don Juan who impassively descends
    The staircase as it drips with infernal splendours.
Not the one who spat at the Law of Moses
    As he sat drinking and sneering with the commander.

His fine eyes have gone unappreciated, have failed to sway hearts;
    And his mouth has known only the kiss of the dream.
And it is he that dreams of her in sombre passion
    And she that disdains him, ceaselessly

Thrusting her chill diamonds and her graveyard lips
    Silent mouth before his mouth and his eyes,
Her sphinx-cruel eyes, animal hands
    Against his eyes and hands, star, heavens

But this man whose heart was murdered by long dead chimeras
    Who keep their addled beaks thrust in his affairs
Can save you on the threshold of judgement day
    If you only give him a live kiss, O you beauties who must pass.

The laughter of his lips shall crush strawberries
    His eyes be marked by a purer destiny
Bacchus reborn out of ashes and embers,
    Ashes in teeth, cinders in hand

But for one reborn how many still living
    Are burdened heart and foot with grievous manacles …
The streams shall continue their flowing and the dead their rotting …
    Each year green leaves shall return to the oak.

When I desire I dwell in a shadowed ravine, the sky over a diamond shredded by the shadow of the fir and the larch and the rocks of the steep slopes.
Through the grass of the ravine strange tubers push columbine and Medea's herbs; and over them fly dragon flies and praying mantises. Sky, flora and fauna are endlessly the same; muskrat and sullen rook pursue insects through them indifferently: so I do not know what timeless season has fallen on this ravine of perpetual night with its bestarred diamond canopy, which no cloud crosses.
On the tree-trunk two initials are carved, and always the same.
By what knife, what heart?
When I first came here the valley was deserted. I was the first there.
No-one else has ever wandered through it.
Frogs swim in the pool and its shadows with regular movement, on it the gleam of the motionless stars; and in the marsh the sonorous, sad cry of the toad: the mood of these places never alters.
It is Love's season, sad, motionless, hovering in this solitude. My love for it shall not end. I shall probably never be able to break through the bordering pines and larches, clamber the baroque rocks and reach the

white road, where at fixed times of day she passes, the road where the shadows do not always fall the same way.

It sometimes seems to me that night has just fallen. Hunters pass on the road I cannot see. The cry of hunting horns carries through the larches. They've had a long day among ploughed fields after fox, deer or badger. The breath of the hounds smokes white in the night.

The hunting songs fade. With difficulty I work out the identical initials on the trunks of the larches that border the ravine.

No star's falling has made the spray to fly: nothing troubles
    The mountains, or the heavens, the flame
Or the waters save this horizontal flighting of feathers
    The fall, and, the death of a bird

And nothing shall stop this feather's flying
    Not the gleaming hair of a barbarian horseman
Not the despised ink at the bottom of the inkwell
    Not the singing wave or the blinding hurricane

Not the seducing necks of the unfortunate ladies of loveliness
    Not the branch of the tree and the shut tomb,
Not the boats that make the night creak with their cables,
    Not the wall where names make hearts

Not the song of the lepers in the bitter marshes
    Not the ice asleep at the bottom of the avenues
Among the trembling ceaseless reflections of the street lamp
    And always, lovely snow, a woman's bare body

Not the great sea monsters with their smoking scales,
    Not the northern fogs with their blue sores,
Not the mirror before which a woman dreams through the evening
    Recalling in memory a future affair

Not the echoing yells of a lost traveller
    Not the wayward cloud, not travelling horses,
Not the shadow of a diver on the quays and bridges
    Or of the paving stone fastened round his neck

Not you Fouquier-Tinville with your hands of clear wax:
> Stars, hands, love, eyes and blood
Seem like rockets rising from a crater. Bye!
> Its morning white as the ocean breaker.

Oh hands that would kill you for love!
> We will know to give you the reddest of baptisms;
And by it shall pale the fires of the great furnaces
> And the sun shall die on the breast of pale fogs

The loveliest eyes of the world have known our thoughts
> We have tried all the well known vices
But kisses and senseless luxury
> Have not extinguished the hope in our grieving hearts.

I saw then gates of crystal open
> On the purer crystal of a wond'rous being.
"Throw in the stream your heart of metal
> And shatter the flasks on the marble tables

Shatter eye and eardrum and as your tongues
> Are to be devoured by the dogs you spat on
Bid farewell to your desires, those pitching boats,
> That your hands and your feet may be murdered by bondage.

Be humble, put by hope in the current of
> Your fears your splendour and your rack
That I may increase your suffering
> Performing exquisite cruelties on you".

It is SHE spoke. It is the loved one too,
> It is the crystal heart, the pitiless eyes,
The most beautiful eyes in the world, oh luminous springs,
> The lovely mouth with its carnivorous teeth.

Thrust both of your hands in my docile brain
> Nibble my lips and pretend to kiss me …
If the strength and the splendour are of easy virtue,
> Hard is the loneliness that is forced on love …

I was talking of a ghost, and of a bird's falling.
    My dreams lose the words that my mouth was using.
This meadow where I am speaking is furrowed with graves
    And the echo of the mallet's clear sound lingers.

In the prison across the way they're making ready the scaffold.
    The condemned man sleeps on his comfortless bed
Dreaming of the great crows who overflew the plain
    That time he met with desire and fear.

These two jealous ghosts were walking side by side
    Catching cloak and face on the branches.
Mercilessly stricken by false lovers because of their fault
    They were making their long pilgrimage in their pursuit.

Fires were whistling on the rooftops of the hamlets.
    Attracted by celestial traps the fish
Were slowly climbing across the branches
    And charcoal burners were leaving their low-thatched cottages.

The condemned man was talking in his sleep to one of them
    More ghostly than the oak where the man was struck.
"Listen" he was saying "to the cattle's distant lowing.
    The wind whispering here will break their fastening".

Listen till day to the voice of the heartless one,
    Her mouth the flavour of a poisoned fruit.
The sky and the mountain, where they call the flocks home
    Have just merged before our astonished eyes.

Enchanted by the birds, and deceived by love,
In corridors of darkness, beneath most shadowy arches
The Lover shall seek no more the mark of the sword
That flame-hearted Iris plunged into his heart …
Blade of perfect thread, sister to mystic streams.

    The bird that sang for her
    In its cage sings no more
    And the queen of the swallows turns
    No more, no more

One day I met with the vulture and the seahawk.
    I was not astonished by their shadow across the earth.
I made out later on ramparts of chalk
    In charcoal the initial of a name I know.

A vampire has smitten my window with his song.
    Crowned with pondweed let him enter
And wearing his lovely necklace of living ladybirds
    To forecast love, the rain and the shine.

> *to sleep with her*
> *to sleep side by side*
> *for the parallel dreamings*
> *for the breathing as one*
>
> *to sleep with her*
> *for the unique and surpassing shade*
> *for the same warmth*
> *for the same solitude*
>
> *to sleep with her*
> *for the dawn shared together*
> *for the same midnight*
> *for the same ghosts*
>
> *to sleep to sleep with her*
> *for the absolute love*
> *for the vice for the vice*
> *for the kisses of every kind*
>
> *to sleep with her*
> *for an unspeakable shipwreck*
> *to prostitute oneself for the other*
> *to lose oneself*
>
> *to sleep with her*
> *to prove oneself and to prove truly*
> *that never has the lie of an original task*
> *pressed on the hearts and bodies of lovers*

always to have the deepest love for her
isn't difficult
but all is dubious for the hearts of fire, for the faithful hearts

always to have the deepest love
are there any involuntary betrayals
no the flesh never lies
and the body of the most vicious stays pure

pure, as the deepest love for her
in my own heart it flourishes without let
no filth ever stained her image
the only love in the heart of the lover

no filth ever stained the deepest love for her
it is for its purity one admires the diamond
no filth stains the diamond or the deepest love for her
the most beloved in the heart of the lover

the sincerest lover capable of the deepest love
is not a monk an ascetic or a puritan
and if he experiences the bodies of the most lovely women
it is because he knows very well the most lovely body is his beloved's

the sincerest lover is a profligate
his mouth has met and dwells on every kind of kiss
should he be indulged in every vice
he only desires more

for the sincerest lover if he isn't loved by the one he loves
it worries him little, he will love her
will eternally desire to be loved
and out of hopeless loving will become pure as diamond

his whole body will be only an elusive quarry
for false women and false affairs
and without pity
the true lover will sacrifice all for her he loves

what does it matter if he has always the deepest love for her
on the day of the longed-for meeting
he will be purer than the dawn and fire
and ready for the ecstasy

always to have the deepest love for her
there is no bodily treason
and how your heart beats always for her
how your eyes are shut on her unique image

to be loved by her
no luck no bliss
no desire even
but will or rather destiny

to be loved by her
not one night of all nights
but forever for the eternal present
without countryside without lights

to be loved by her
written in the signs of the time
despite all contrary past and future
forever

but to be loved by her
it becomes necessary to lose all but love

Life let us not speak of it —

Of Love — no more of that either

to be loved by her
is inevitable
no songs no shouts
no false feeling

to be loved by her
impassable marble congealed seas implacable skies
but waiting waiting long time waiting again
waiting? denied by Eternity

to die after her
is the role that falls to the lover
his supreme right
to carve a name on a stone that will perish

to carve a name on a tree that will perish
and to be extinguished forever

to be snuffed out himself after her
but love the deepest love
will burn as an eternal flame

How many long months my dear since I first loved you
    Why no desire to know my works?
If my days are subject to gloomy routines
    My nights are escorted by noble marshals.

Must I again preside over the bonfire's resurrection
    — So hot the Phoenix couldn't survive there —
Or, shipwrecked, toss senselessly towards
    Passing ships the pages of this book?

Must I be destroyed to extinguish my faith?
    My dream's universe exalts your image
But the legendary lands I have made for you
    Is there a better way of crossing them than through your mirage?

If it is necessary to die at the foot of rival idols
    I am ready. Admitting only your cruel splendour
I will die if you like, so, to become in your annals
    Merely the fading echo of a useless passion

I give everything up for you, even into the heart of the phantoms.
    Prisoner to this fatal delicious torment
Am ready to disappear in two lines of a book
    And without being invoked of an evening by lovers.

I am weary of fighting a fate that eludes,
    Weary of trying to forget, of remembering
Every slight scent from your dress
    Weary of hating you and of blessing you.

I deserved better of you, but you did not understand
    One day of seashore sunshine on the rocks
Remember the lover who gave you his heart's truth
    And strove to serve you, fearless, beyond reproach.

Do you wait for me to land on faraway shores
    Sighing as you look at your deserted knees
"So who is it who's gone away. I don't know his face;
    But why is he going away alone towards his freedom?

He must be found again must this faithless slave
    To be punished, then chained in my dungeon
To serve me once more with model heart
    And even his pain shall not touch my pity

For I am masterful; and I desire to be obeyed.
    Nothing shall leave me without permission.
As for whoever it is who's returning to my service
    If he has not put by his haughty pride

I know of fantastic prisons for hearts.
    May the renegade lover return as soon as possible:
I need plenty of servants for this evening
    To clean my shoes and to hand me my cloak".

What good is it. The escaped convict is well acquainted with his prison.
    He has certainly chosen too precious hostages
To want once again to pay you ransom:
    The treasures of pure hearts do not suffer division.

Keep yourself free from ocean's powers and prisons.
    Goodbye. Myself I'll go as one dies — in the dawning.
Miles shall not make the distance but the words
    "I used to love her" murmured afar.

Adorable sign written in the dead waters
Muddy depths
O fish who prowl about the weed
Where is the spring I have heard flowing so long and which I've never come to
Who ceaselessly shuts heavy clanging gates
Dead waters unseen spring
Criminals wait for me where the path turns among the great hemlocks
Like the clouds the evenings are senselessly born and die with this tattooing above the left breast: tomorrow
The water slowly flows through a crack in the bottle where the most famous astrologers come to drink the elixir of life
While the man with the shut eyes knows only to keep on saying
"A stork lost, two refound".
And the hemlocks droop in the shade of the meeting place
And how tomorrow punctually but disguised as an honest man or a great red umbrella opens in the middle of the prairie where the farmers' wives of the Dawn dry their washing
Ghastly ghostlike statues of marble erected in Night's palaces

A blade of justice cracks
A splinter creaks in the floor
A sword falls unaided and sticks in the floor
And I walk without stopping across a succession
Of large empty rooms whose polished floors reflect like water
There are hands in this night of the marsh
A white hand and one which is like a living being
Which is the hand I would place my lips on and where I dare not put them
There are horrible hands
The melancholy schoolboy's hand black with ink
The gory hand on the wall of the room where the crime was committed
The hand pallid with death
Hands holding a knife or a revolver
    Open hands
    Shut hands
Submissive hands holding pens
O my hand you too, you too
My hand with your lines and moreover it's then . . .
Why stain your mysterious lines

Why? Rather handcuffs rather mutilate yourself rather rather
Write write for it's a letter to her that you're writing and this impure way a
 way of touching her
Hands outstretched hands that offer yourselves
Is there a sincere hand among them
Ah I no longer dare shake hands
Lying hands dastardly hands hands I hate
Hands that swear true affection and tremble when I look at the eyes
Is there yet a hand I can shake with confidence

    Hands on the loving mouth
    Hands on the loveless heart
    Hands on the loving fire
    Hands whose false love cuts
    Hands heavy upon Love
    Hands dead to Love
    Hands forced for Love
    Hands lifted against Love
    Hands grasping at Love
    Hands high against Love
    Hands stretched towards Love
    Hands of Love's works
    Hands happy from Love
    Hands in the dough outside Love's horrible hands

    Hands eternally linked by Love
    Hands washed by Love by implacable waves
    Hands in hands it is Love who prowls
    Full hands it is Love again
    Hands of the soldier it is the true Love
    Mother's hands hands of Love
    Hand offered to Love
    Hand of Justice hand of Love
    Hand strong in Love

    Hands hands every hand

A man drowns himself a hand comes out of the waves
A man goes away a hand is troubled
A hand is wrinkled a heart suffers
A hand is hurt O anger of Gods
A hand again a hand
A hand on my shoulder
Who is it?

Is it you at last?
It is getting too dark. What shadows
I no longer know who the hands belong to
What they want
What they say
The hands are deceptive
I remember again white hands stretched out in the darkness on a table in the
    waiting room
I remember hands whose embrace was dear to me
And I know no more
There are too many betrayers too many liars
Ah even my hand that writes
A knife! A weapon! A tool
Everything except writing
Blood for blood

Patience! Day shall come

Wild rose withered in the grass
O yellow leaves
All cracks in this room
As in the night-walk grasses under the feet
Huge invisible wings paralyse my arms and the roar of a far-off sea reaches me

The bed rolls till dawn its border of spray and dawn does not come
Will never come.
Crushed glass, rotted wood panelling, endless dreams, faded blooms
A hand moves through the shadows. purely white, on to my brow
For the bird of paradise flying knocking itself on the walls and furniture, the
    bird I've shut up through carelessness
And I will listen till the improbable day
Nothing but in shutting the eyes

Never the Dawn to great cries making blue the washing boards,
The Dawn, soap diluted in the water of black streams,
The Dawn will not froth upon this ghastly night
Nor upon our trembling fingers or our empty glasses
It is the night that has no frontier, daughter of fir trees
That makes the grapnel's chain groan at the door
Night of loveless nights Strangler of the Dream
Bloody night night of fire night of war that has no truce
Night of the way lost amid the stairs
And of feet once more treading too heavily on the landings
Luxurious night of fall into the depth
Night of chains rattling in the room of the crime
Night of naked phantoms gliding into the beds
Night of awaking when the sleepers are made feeble
Feeling the blood foaming in their thin chests
And the foam of the spasm mounting to their teeth
They fondle through the dark a hairy vampire
And are unable to tell if the greedy monster
Is not their own heart beating beneath their grubby sides.
Night of indistinct echoes and dampened embers
Night of fires sparkling on the mirrors
Night of blindness fumbling for coins in drawers
Night of loveless nights when the sheets slip away
When the police start whistling on the boulevards
O night! cruel night when nightdresses shiver
And voices whisper at the bedside of the sick,
Night, closed forever by bolts of steel
Night, solitary night, starless, harbourless!
In your eyes, in your heart, in the sky too
See suddenly lighting up the imprecise Universe
The fissure swelling, narrow, full of light
As if some wild beast with languid claws
Had embraced night and torn it apart
(But the light shall be pale and slow the tide)
Ribs rushing into the delicacy of the crystal
Cracks mimicking snakes' agility
Who would rush and become tangled in the light
Pale with a strange dawn. Then when the player

Tired of turning over the cards and their symbols
Sees the cruel morning lighting up the doorways
Many the thoughts nearly forgotten with the tears of desire
And many the faded fans that fall on the landings

   Quiet. Let the pen rest; and shut up your ears
      To the slow heavy steps on the stairs,
   The night grows pale now: but this dawn is like
      Dead moths at the feet of candlesticks

   A storm of phantom sacrifices are your eyes
      As they defy them with the steel of desire.
   The sky is more faded than a photograph worn by much looking
      And desires only a rest.

   Call Star and Siren with great cries
      — If you cannot sleep with mouth closed and hands joined —
   Like a stone horseman smiling to see
      Heaven godless and Hell without remorse

   O break forth!

Michel Deguy

RURAL REMNANTS

1

   Never was ghost so tenacious; put more cunning, was more dogged in the pursuit of pointless obsession; never more determined to imitate the back and forth flux of the elemental; to become elemental man, obsessed with Universe; to return, wounding trees, sky and sea; making itself an obstacle, directing administration of silence to all limits whence returns, finishes, tireless wave, tireless bird, tireless sea; interposed between sand and spray, cliff and storm, field edge and corn ear, He, the revenant, everywhere substituting himself for that which hurts another, so gaining capability of blessing; He, the being of the borders, elevating his house to the confluence of the valley and the plain, beaten, broken, by the moraines of alluviums as by lava, jammed in crossroads of moraines of the snow storm and the forest; but reborn with day with no hate for the things of violence, more aware of the mine and the typhoon, the avalanche and the well, that break themselves to bury him.

2

Moreover they died in great numbers like algae in ocean depth
They died in clusters as the grape in the vat
They died as jellyfish on the open shore
As if cousins and brothers had been born
Just to invent these fresh hecatombes
An unbelievable way to make us die

Their eyes of night and mist the road menders
Carbonised the stone heaps with the dead skins
All in november among the debris of the chestnuts

And everywhere
She of Bavaria, of Saxony and of Prussia
Where the villages have the names of slaughter houses.

3
The heart
Well it's like a farm kitchen
In August after vespers
Deep, and lukewarm, and feeling the snot
Where the phrasemonger flies harass
With riddles of honey, and of cherry, and cold blood

The heart
Well that's like an immortal heath
Where the dogs search out the fat pheasants
The heart
Well it's like Don Quixote
Swearing but a bit late he isn't going to be taken in anymore
He moults and drops hairs in his bed
He's had his bedroom decorated
With a wallpaper that's got windmills on

4   THE STORM APPROACHES
When the thick clouds lead in the night
Just before his hour
When road meets with horizon of fog
Before the horizon
When the willows are quiet and shiver in the silence
Before the coming of the wind
When odd drops of moisture deliciously wound the eyes
Before the falling of the rain
When mystery makes black the dog

5   EVENING

The waterclocks and the reedwalls
Drip
Eleven strokes sound in the moon
The cats are afraid of porcelain

Then — and without breaking the night's snoring
It glides into the woodcut of the alders
And among the boxtrees
The vocal chords of the stream have spoken

From here one sees inside
On the screen of the frontages the magic lanterns of Japanese meals
And children asleep
And disturbed women hanging themselves
But burglary does not yield the inside
And the thief outside the house is turned away

From next door though he'll get his rest
For she is fast in the hollow memory that she pierces
And the man penetrated
Shall dwell in his proper depth:
Here lie the memorable evenings
When the greatest grief hung on her home
And to prepare for it
Made itself precede separations and griefs

6

    When there was only those long and passing days, the disdain of praise and the lofty watch against injustice — and the morning in tatters at the window — and the flappings of live trees beneath the axes of trains

    When there was only the upright man, vowed to the day, centred on skin, waiting for the cutting edge of the winds to make the heart weak — in the spasm of the words a heart that reneges on itself

    And the bridge caved in to a slight river to stop the crossing for the first time, and on the opposite bank a rusted gate that the clinging brambles padlocked again, stopped access a second time

    But when there would have been only this: the child's joy at the first break of day; and the adult delight in refinding love when it was lost: when the topsoil stood bare without the night's jewelling

7

All was fulfilled — and already he leaves his furtive watch
Already he dies with the others, under the gray flagstones of the clouds,
    the buried one;
Heaven recloses the vault. The earth is the tomb. He has come there to die
He is there for nothing
Always he hurtles into delay
The mighty storms race upon the sea unexpected
Here and there under the arch of the sunclouds by the gaps of the trellis
Between the huge vines of violet cloud and swaying sun stem the great
    nenuphar of the sea stirs
Being come at last, preceded by great beasts?

Michel Deguy

from OUI DIRE

Poet of profile
Poet of square body and shadow on thresholds
Poet Gulliver delineating a bramble in winter with Hopkins' pencil
Or waning to bring the grass in the garden in accordance with the compass
    of Gongora
Genie out of persian tales because he says no to indifference

He maintains the blue lymph in the tracery of the elms
Vigil over — zeta epsilon delta of Orion on the low branch
Triple set eye from witch one witch two witch three
That flies away subtle crow constellation

He is here to invent something lovely as a word, saxifrage, that nobody invented
If he hunts a treasure he finds it
(Imagine a fish hunting a fish in the shadowiness of the seas)

When he returns among us into the transparence of Winter where things are lines
When he reopens the vein of colours in the open mine of heaven
When he returns on the narrow hospitable dyke
And victorious splits the coagulated earth knowing
That life slips away a small distance
When he gets back his totem in balls the colour of excrement
Among the little french apple trees near where they keep the ploughshares
And when pushed on the shoulders as by one born again
He follows the river having an invitation to the Mill
And the cock with his comb of lilacs and his voice that carries
    The blind one gloves himself with willow
    And sets his back to the river
    And gropingly, hand outstretched
    Advances through a strange world
He hurries towards the desert plateau where church spire is sundial
The void is his power The sun slips away like a wedding ring
Among the plenitude of trees he belongs to deceit
Emigré an age scalps he strives for his love who is absent, who is under
               his feet and sleeps when he wakes

To regain the lost one of his land who wakes when he sleeps
Time is that which has no thinking of her

He emigrated to Winter and its pious branches
Winter made manifold in signal fashion
Bones woods and width, steps voices and space occupied with the journeyings of
 justice
Spying on the visible where the voices know transformation
He emigrated from clutching vein pipe
Syrinx throttled and hollow voices gathered before him
Where blood makes longer his pain, heart going against ear

They would make him king!
 The clients of the Wind grasp at him
Their shouts bear him
 Each voice demands a fresh hearing
Winter rehearses the cases
A group of flowers waits its turn
There are these scrofulas from the edge of the forest There are these ruins
Yoke and singed buffalo's forehead
 How did you come to ruin?

The crasis of hands alleviates to left and right
A stone waited a hundred thousand years He grants the desire of the flints
A toy of ebony on furrow that is different from it
For the "Adunata" left the dream and came to earth
All that is real is possible
The fables speak as animals

Shade of Virgil become voice of Virgil
Voice of Muse become desire and obedience
I am you listening to the cry that gives voice to brotherly Hell, I listen
 to your headless voice attentive to the silence that does
 not cease beneath the trellis and resembles the avenger
 plotting vengeance

I recognise suffering thanks to places
The grass was not his growing The beast has remained
You I listen to you What did you say of your season?
I descend the valley sharingly
              A leaf
Climbs back up towards the village

The ricks of bones Let us reassemble them in the fire
The wrong? But man yields you room
Have the birds highways? Let this boundary be removed
May water dry up in this usurped place
      Unknot the tangles of these straggling acacias
          Softly remove the blue cosmos
              That is held by the palisades of winter

The streams   The view
The slopes   The bundle of paths
He steers us towards a bed of syllables

The wind's his whip
He favours transhumance from land to land
Calls noise muttering of soils
Following the arc where Heaven
Has centred its lights
Word Cypresses then
That rise and swing

By these that march into a galaxy of the open mine of heaven (props of elm
         and pillars of sandstone, soil of earth and sky of heaven)
            by these that utter
Behold by the forest edge
The world in need of proclamation
"The kingdom resembles for example this road
Beyond the deep wall of this iron-grilled castle
The kingdom resembles this place
That requires a parabola for home"

Table

Paul Valéry	TOMBS BY THE SEA	5
Louis Aragon	LILACS AND ROSES 1940	10
Rene Char	ARTINE	11
	THE SHE OF HISTORY	13
	FORCE OF MILDNESS	14
	THE TOR	15
	CUR SECESSISTI	16
	ANGUISH, EXPLOSION, SILENCE	17
	PENUMBRA	18
Robert Desnos	THE NIGHT OF LOVELESS NIGHTS	19
Michel Deguy	RURAL REMNANTS	37
	from OUI DIRE	41

ACKNOWLEDGEMENTS

Some of these versions appeared in magazines or books published by, Xenia Press, The Lace Curtain, University of Salzburg Press, etruscan reader IX (Fred Beake, Nicholas Moore, Meg Bateman), Mammon Press, Spiny Babbler and South West Review.

Rene Char: the versions are taken from *Fureur et Mystere* (Gallimard 1962), *Les Matinaux* (Gallimard 1950), *Le Marteau Sans Maitre* (Jose Corti, 1934).

Michel Deguy: the versions are taken from *Poemes 1960-70* (Gallimard 1973).

Robert Desnos: *The Night of Loveless Nights* is from *Fortunes* (Gallimard 1942).

Louis Aragon: the poem is from *Le Crevecoeur* (NRF 1941).

Paul Valéry: the poem is from *Poesies* (NRF 1929).

© Fred Beake 2005

This edition © etruscan books 2005

ISBN
1 901538 55 8 paper

etruscan books
28 Fowlers Court
Fore Street
Buckfastleigh
South Devonshire
ENGLAND
TQ11 0AA

etruscan@macunlimited.net
www.e-truscan.co.uk

typography: Robert Moore
robert.moore@zetnet.co.uk

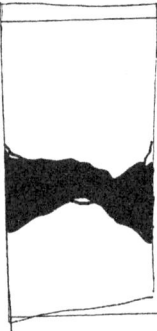

exhibition

Brian Catling	*Lost Harping: last century works*
Bob Cobbing	*Shrieks & Hisses: Selected Poems vol 16*
Bob Cobbing	*kob bok: collected poems 1944-99*
Nicholas Johnson (ed.)	*Foil: defining poetry 1985-2000*
Tom Leonard	*Intimate Voices: Selected work 1965-83*
Tom Leonard	*access to the silence: work 1985-2000*
Maggie O'Sullivan	*red shifts*
Maggie O'Sullivan	*Waterfalls*
Carlyle Reedy	*EPOS*
Maurice Scully	*5 freedoms of movement*
Iain Sinclair	*Saddling the Rabbit*

etruscan readers

I	Helen Macdonald, Gael Turnbull, Nicholas Johnson
II	Tom Scott, Sorley MacLean, Hamish Henderson
III	Maggie O'Sullivan, David Gascoyne, Barry MacSweeney
IV	Bob Cobbing, Maurice Scully, Carlyle Reedy
V	Tom Raworth, Bill Griffiths, Tom Leonard
VI	Robin Blaser, Barbara Guest, Lee Harwood
VII	Alice Notley, Wendy Mulford, Brian Coffey
VIII	Douglas Oliver, Tina Darragh, Randolph Healy
IX	Fred Beake, Nicholas Moore, Meg Bateman

etruscan books

Edward Dorn	*High West Rendezvous : a Sampler*
Bill Griffiths	*A Book of Spilt Cities*
John Hall	*else / here: new & selected poems*
Nicholas Johnson	*CLEAVE*
Nicholas Johnson	*Pelt*
Nicholas Johnson	*Show*
Helen Macdonald	*Shaler's Fish*
Stuart Montgomery	*Islands*
Wendy Mulford	*and suddenly, supposing : Selected Poems*
Maggie O'Sullivan	*WATERFALLS*
Tom Pickard	*fuckwind*
Carl Rakosi	*The Earth Suite*
Carl Rakosi	*The Old Poet's Tale: Collected Works vol 1*
Seán Rafferty	*Poems*
Seán Rafferty	*Poems, Revue Sketches and Fragments*
Harriet Tarlo	*NAB*